On the Way to the Beach

BY HENRY COLE

Greenwillow Books
An Imprint of HarperCollins Publishers

To my mother,
who loved to sit
and watch the ocean

On the Way to the Beach
Copyright © 2003 by Henry Cole
All rights reserved.
Manufactured in China.
www.harperchildrens.com

Acrylic paints were used
to prepare the full-color art.
The text type is Kabel.

Library of Congress
Cataloging-in-Publication Data

Cole, Henry.
On the way to the beach / by Henry Cole.
        p.   cm.
"Greenwillow Books."
Summary: A visit to the beach brings
encounters with various creatures
of nature. Flaps fold out to reveal
the plants and animals on each
two-page spread.
ISBN 0-688-17515-5
1. Toy and movable books—Specimens.
[1. Seashore animals—Fiction. 2. Nature—Fiction.
3. Toy and movable books.] I. Title.
PZ7.C67345 On 2001   [E]—dc21   99-086871

First Edition 10 9 8 7 6 5 4 3 2 1

 Greenwillow Books

One summer morning
I went for a walk to the beach.
I followed the path
through the woods. . . .

I sat very still in the
sassafras beneath
a loblolly pine.
I saw . . .

I wandered out of the woods
and into a salt marsh.
I wonder who's watching me?

a snowy egret

salt marsh fleabane

tracks in mud

a marsh fiddler crab

salt marsh periwinkles

a coot taking off

a mosquito

a marsh hawk

a clapper rail at its nest

a diamondback terrapin

hite ibis

salt marsh skipper butterfly

I followed a sandy trail
that led to a dune.
I wonder who's watching me?

I sat near the dune and listened to the breeze whooshing through the sea oats.

I saw . . .

I sat on the damp sand
of the beach and
smelled the salt air.
I saw . . .